DEFORMATIONS

Sasha Dugdale is a poet and translator. She has published four collections of poetry with Carcanet. Her fourth collection, *Joy*, was a PBS Choice in 2017, the title poem having won the Forward Prize for Best Single Poem in 2016.

also by Sasha Dugdale

Joy
Red House
The Estate
Notebook

SASHA DUGDALE

Deformations

CARCANET

First published in Great Britain in 2020 by
Carcanet
Alliance House, 30 Cross Street
Manchester M2 7AQ
www.carcanet.co.uk

A CIP catalogue record for this book is
available from the British Library.

ISBN 978 1 78410 898 4

Book design by Andrew Latimer
Printed in Great Britain by SRP Ltd, Exeter, Devon

The publisher acknowledges financial
assistance from Arts Council England.

for the insignificant

CONTENTS

HEADLAND

PITYSAD

it can feel wrong
that it never is doves
themselves impassively
writing of doves...

— *from* alphabet *by Inger Christensen,*
translated by Susanna Nied

GIRL AND HARE

There was once a girl and she had a hare
as a pet. It was so long and brown and soft.
It stretched its body next to hers on the sunlounger
where she lay in her oversized sunglasses,
little and freckled. The hare had the tautness of game
its hindquarters were round and solid
but she could nest its paws in her hand
ring them with her fingers as a poacher might
       but tenderly.
When the sun was bright she could see through
       the hare's hindlegs,
its thin skin, thrown hurriedly over bone and tendon,
the light pulsed red and sombre as if the hare
       itself contained
a small convex sun like a red blood cell.
Hare had a narrow breast like hers, rosed with fur,
       and little childish shoulders
but forearms like a strong man's,
       the sinews and fibres twanging
       soundlessly
as it shifted.
Now it lay still, although hares never sleep, its lip moving
       gently and its amber eyes
       waxing and waning.
It lowered its lids, for a moment it looked sly, knowing.
Hare is apparently drowsing. The girl removes her glasses,
       places them on hare's face
and closes her eyes.
This is hare's moment: as long as her, and as old.

WELFARE HANDBOOK

A female peacock would be a monstrosity
what shape would it assume? How hard it is
to envisage a building that goes up and up.
When I write about this, shall I bang my fist
on the pound of paper to puncture it
or shall I gradually entrap my subject
with words written in mucus and the outgoings,
in discharge, in dirty things like cleaning cloths,
retreating onto the sands of flirtation
where masculinity is exhausted
prickled by marram and saltbush
dragging the long shaft of his cross.

Wondering about a sign here, shall I pick
a cross with four decorative dots to signify
face to face (on top) or a simple x, sideways,
generally from back. No sign is left now
every typographic glyph looks labial,
the asterisk may make a light shine
but nowadays I see only a/hole
for the obelus to cut and pierce.

Think of a utopian city
Think of its binding walls and its symmetry
The age of attack and repulse is past
but the sympathetic walls remain
purposeful (unlike those sprawling lines of slums
that rise like scales over the downs).
Think how all have a function in this city
And are dressed in different colours:
ultramarine, lead tin yellow, verdigris.
We work hard, but when we are not working
we congregate in profile against arcades
and fall in love with the truth.

Some are bakers, some butchers,
some are makers of shoes, or windows, or brushes.
The streets are harmonious, they smell of woodshavings
rising bread, and cake. Women assist the
slaughter of pigs, the curing of parts.

Every so often a prophet opens a top window
Or an angel lowers itself like a stagehand.
A baby is born at intervals and placed in a trough
for safekeeping.

At the same time (I learn on a walk)
men on battle cruisers, serving in the gun turrets
often died of burns that were
invisible. Their white bodies were spared:
the nobility of the unflawed body
(especially when poverty had clothed it vulgarly)
on the morgue table
combusting rather than decomposing,
a clearness clouded over with flame
a flickering along the uncharred bough.
Measure limbs with a footrule
measure all parts. Measure member.

Why add to the shimmering slithering mess in the warehouse? Why scrape the plate? Throw away nothing. Wear clothes until they become clots of felt in the soil. Say nothing. Never cut a hair on your head. Never shave. Welcome the emission, the fluorescence, the excrescence. Shuffle on your knees, like the old women climbing the stones to the Weeping Madonna. Prostrate yourself in front of the sun and the sun's son. As many stinking binbags as there are grains of sand on the shore at Cyrene, between the oracle of sultry Jupiter and the Tomb of Old Battus, perhaps a private beach now, or maybe a launch point for inflatable dinghies? As many cotton buds as there are stars in the sky to behold the illicit fumblings of men in railway carriages.

an experiment

a chapel in the house
a place for the loom
a black slate shelf for butter
a basket for pine cones
a vase of foxgloves
a measuring rule
a pile of stones
a railway bank
a handful of daughters
a kettle for tea
a sheep-coloured coat
a whetstone a snath
a pony and trap
a young woman
a young woman
a daughter
an old woman
a spaniel

skivvies are always open to sex
but are inordinately modest about their bodies
their nipples their sexes always wrapped in membranes
in sackcloth in ashes in integuments
their billowing pubic hair
curling like a signature behind drawers drawstrings
undrawn but dreamed of
they grab your hand with their dirty fingers and lead it
up into the warm space
the stink of those scrubbers and their sex saliva
if you rip them open they black your eye

sex with children upsets us
more than it used to. As my friend's mother
once pointed out: stay away from him
you know what he's like. They're manipulative
said the policeman, they often ingratiate themselves
with the parents, it's never a one-off.
At the assizes, name in the papers,
three youths, no more than kids,
threw eggs and tomatoes so the jelly
slid down your lapel. The prohibition
is like a seawall in the adult mind, but back then
the waters slopped in and out the harbour.
Slamming the steering wheel he said well what the
fuck do you want me to do about it? Punch his face?
Sullen are the righteous, the attentive fingers of luminaries
are never seen by them, those lonely exquisite pickings:
at most risk the anxious child who fears not pleasing
who says, yes yes I love you, who learns pleasure
is a structure like a tent, erected on sand
pack it up take it with you
it will never catch you unawares.

angelus at 6 but before that the fire is lit
and he brings up a cup of tea
and perhaps he kisses her brow or strokes it
I am surprised at your vehemence when you say
this act is the most evil of all
but I understand now,
because in that offering of tea and the chaste kiss
he makes the unthinkable consistent with the thinkable.

Love, that slippery snake, is like the law
it eats its nether eye with its morning mouth.
Don't think of the nights and they will be slotted
neatly into stacks of cups on planed shelves.
If he entered you and it hurt then it was done
gently, with the best intentions

ME AS BRIDE OF CHRIST AT ST GEORGE'S

A whole procession of us, white-robed,
even white shoes and socks.
I wore my mother's wedding veil, studded with pearls
for Corpus Christi Day. A day like today
a hayfever day, the meadows' first cut
and the bees, the roses out, everything ripe.
The priest, noticing our bad habits,
said we must never keep the wafer in our mouth
as it is the body of Christ, but we vied
for who could suck the longest.
My grandmother took photos on a polaroid
and in all of them our heads cut off
just our young torsos bobbing towards the chapel.

SEXUAL ANTINOMIANISM

O St Euph, patron saint of euphemism
for you the mysteries will be rewritten:
the mystery of the stolen virgin, or try
the mystery of the silent nights when
the mysteries of sex were illuminated
and they turned out to be the usual
mechanical insults. The mystery of the shift
diaphanous and yet chaste, the plaits, oh
the mystery of hair and the mystery (for some)
of why two sisters might have begged the youngest
to marry without delay, to do secretarial, to become
a governess, or to drown herself perhaps,
when they left home with their husbands.

mental breakdown is often pictured as a wasteland
but this is a false analogy. Just picture the deserts
of Mexico, blooming with cactuses like prosthetic limbs.
A wasteland is what we have been taught to fear,
unhusbanded, without the city walls, infertile
cracking up, seams undoing themselves in the dry earth.

DIRECT CARVING

Looking up
the hotel mirror
caught a shape brief
in its oblong
before it settled
of a woman dirty white
stone thigh up
on the bed
Heavy right angle
of marbled planes
the light of a gallery
on her crown
She was bent her shoulders
rounded breasts rounded
She was applying
cream glinting on the scar
of her tibia her hands
seemed to clasp her calf
She radiated no light
a cold star burnt
in her uterus
Then I recognised her
I'd seen her before but
didn't know her name

White poplars are green until they suddenly flip
into trees of tiny white flags in the breeze.
Like that doll, whose skirt, carefully lifted
upended over her head like a bellflower,
revealed a different face, a different outfit,
a different girl existing between the legs of the first

Lawks   high jinks   right and proper naughtiness
a get-up   nooks and crannies   four square
the line to take in this business   india rubber
buttons   am I mad   little by little
cut a tombstone   went with a woman
cold as fishes   this must stop

ONE X FOR MARY AND XX FOR MAY

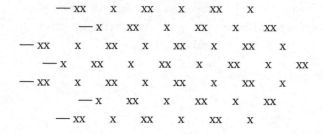

AN INTERVIEW WITH THE KEEPER

We spoke at length about the beast
How in the wild he would have been destroyed
By predators, alternatively
Might have starved, become susceptible to small infections
Open wounds in his fine hide.
Truly the maker of this beast is a genius
He burned so bright on the fields and in the valleys.
If it is possible to say of a beast: he had imagination
He had vitality. Even in his cage he is proud.
There are no shortage of admirers.

But, says his keeper, I can't help looking into the flaming
Depths. I glance in, then away. I bring him food
But I can hardly bear to look him in the face.
Behold him, then shrivel. Shrivel, stretch and weep.
Look and look away. This is the pattern of my guardianship.
I turn my pictures to the wall. I have no mirrors.
I talk into the night about my Janus neck,
Supporting two heads, two sets of eyes,
My conjoined sensibilities, the heavy key of the cage.
Sometimes, I continued, I feel that I am the beast
And I am confined. Sometimes, I finished, I feel
The seaspray of spittle on my neck as I shovel,
And it is me spitting.

Eyes averted always, best in profile
shackled in flatness, every image a removal,
taken from her, denied her, peeled off
like dead skin, transparent, but ribbed with her features.
She helped him by divesting herself of an image
he helped her by pulling it down her legs
Come into my hands, come in my hand
He makes a rose of his fingers, in the centre a rasp.

TRANSLATIONS

A garden enclosed is my sister

A locked rock garden and a sealed spring

My sister is a garden that is locked

My sweetheart is a closed garden

A fountain closed off to all others

A garden inclosed is my sister

A spring shut up a fountain sealed

Why do perpetual motion machines never work?
Because history only travels in one direction.
And here we are, considering how the purity of an image
     makes one think
of *a great civilisation where frightening technical skill*
for a rare moment is the free instrument
of the highest sensitivity. So embraces, contortions,
lascivious women, members erect and flaccid
emerge like Pompeii's walls from the rubble of a disaster
and are cleansed by water. *For English is a language of water*
and good for recording disaster.

(quotes from David Jones's obituary of Eric Gill in *The Tablet*,
30 November 1940, and Valerie Meyer Caso's *The Blue Novel*,
translated by Michelle Gil-Montero)

HEADLAND

HEADLAND

Waxy sporadic grass knitting the sand…

A loudspeaker on a car proceeds slowly up the far quay
and a wedge of sandpipers lifts in fright from the shore:
The circus king is back for one last stand!
Last performance of the season – tonight!

His old gardening jacket hangs like a phantom behind the door
I have a febrile energy for undoing endings
tying the old twine to new twine, so when he came to me
   in a dream
and asked to come back I was surprised
to find myself rejecting him one last time

pouring myself a solitary drink of seawater
and reminding him of how we saw the old vessel of his body
and it was no longer fit-for-purpose
could not be recycled or rewound
like string, or green glass, or driftwood.

The whole place reeks of him, who in life smelt of railways
sugar soap and the commuter tang. Sand, salt,
thrift and rotting wrack, and stubbornness:
a vast firewood stack, a few elderly tools revived
with rags and oily fingers to massage working parts,

string tied into rolls of barbed wire.
I am walking today on the hollow old dune
September chill, the children are off buying shoals
of pencils and the circus cut-outs on the sand bank
are blanketed up for the year.

What are years? They last no longer than the tide.
I read the tables, I pore over them and seem to find relief
in the mathematical appearance of water
and how by degrees it creeps upon us,
another ten metres to swill around the back gate.

Last performance of nostalgia out here, where it burns
with an acrid smell. Throw on an armful of regret, it fires up
odd-flamed like rubber or plastic flotsam
or household chemicals glugging themselves empty.
My fingers smell like his.

PIGMENT

I always go to yellow to fight death – Sean Scully

I always go to red to fight insomnia
and blue to fight addiction, and green
feeds my need for approval. But the semitones –
they get under my skin, the nipple pink of palimpsest
sage for the menopause navy blue for rape
grey for greased rope and buttercream for infanticide

the ochres give me a long history of antisemitism
and when they flare and crumble then I see battlefields
no, not red, but violet-black is the mortal colour
sparrow brown is the day dawning on the field
mint green beds the broken flints. I always go to
gold to feel disgust and desire: the desert road
planked with barracks is gold, mucus is dirt gold
corn is tooth gold, but scythed it yields to ash

When a train passes I crouch down on the embankment
to watch the uniform black stars raining on the ballast
Fight exile with indigo, gauze white, and the maroon weal
of an old wound. When I go to yellow
it is the debased colour of survival, sulphurous,
bankrupt and sometimes tinged with a green
that borders on darkness. Darkness is a hymn
I go to when I wish to fight light, when
reasonable light shovels itself
brick red over all the cities and hills
and the clouds look like dust, which looks like
smoke

ROSARIES IN THE SAND

Say a rosary for María and Juana and Guadalupe
also for Ricardo, Jorge, Javier and Carlos
especially the last who sat in wet pants for hours
although was it urine or tears, no one could say.
He's got a burning wish. Something cheap and sugary
but he can't remember anymore, it belongs to another boy.

All the rosary beads are curled in the sand like tiny snakes
And some are rattled and scattered on the asphalt
and the only god is scratchy, wondering why no one can count
and no one's prayers are threaded right. Come on, he says,

five lots of ten, it's like press ups or squats, you train and you get better
come on, you spiritual savages. Where are your glory be's?
But the only sound is sobbing, like beads plopping into puddles
although there are no puddles and no beads.

Come on says god, fingering his arse. I bought you people rosaries
and you drop them in the desert like losers. Gather them up
says god, picking his nose. Put them in your pockets.
I order you, says god. Sometimes by losing a battle
you win a scrap, notes god, taking out a vanity mirror.
He's lost interest now, and he opens a small knife,
cleans his nails of grease and wipes the dirty blade on his hair.

The downs are certainly lovely, although by mortal
    loveliness
did you mean they would disappear one day? They are the
    eternal
feminine, to be walked over, and in and under, they are
    heaven,
they are rifle ranges, and rusting tanks, they are long
    summer bostals
burning magnesium-white, ecstatic lovers under hawthorn,
they are raves and summer parties, dewponds painstakingly
lined with clay, they are dykes, fortifications and man-
oeuvres, they are G.I. brides and land girls, they are poor
land for grazing, rampions, man orchids, they are marked
by monks with crosses, marked with horses and men, the
turf is covered in oily black sheep droppings, battle lines,
beacons, they are military objects, cremated Sikh soldiers,
barbed-wire-land, they are inhabited by lone men, they are
shortcuts and gas pipes and cyclists balanced on the pedals,
they are sheepsheared, rabbitrun, buzzarded, bearded with
old men, topped by trig points and aerials and car parks,
up and down they go, stiled and gated, hare-lipped, still
timeless in summer when the gorse darkens before the sky
as if the sun slept in it and smelt of coconut. They are the
slow misery of D-of-E-ers, charity walkers, daytrippers,
teen daughters. Their backs wear thin like wedding velvet
worn at a funeral, quarries, pylons, swifts, swallows, skylarks,
girls on pony treks and old women who want to die here,
and have brought cake and a deckchair

The contents of the museum were moved to a bunker
and then disappeared. Old photos show us what was lost
a few black-and-white Old Masters taken at a distance

a grainy picture of a statue, hunched, ready for flight
the parure of a lost queen on a throat of ancient velvet.
Even the urge to speculate on their fate is muted now:

shipped out wrapped in sack, burnt or heaped over
with the gravel and rock of a dying city. The odd leads
trail into darkness, which is where the other nine-tenths

of human endeavour end. The known world expands
but the world we buried grows faster still. Its statuary fills
a universe of mirrored halls, its songs echo soundlessly,

and tangled in the stars a thousand poets whose faces
lie smashed under battlefields. As we seek to perfect
the chord, the line, the divine form, remember

wax tablets, scrolls, scribbles on palace walls
trampled into strata, remember how porcelain
melted, remember there's an undone precedent

for everything we've done. Somewhere dark energy
is shooting coins from forgotten civilisations
into a jukebox larger than the sun.

GOLDEN AGE

The child born in the last century
ran along the streams of his childhood
the hedgerows of hazel and plum
and in winter he pressed closer to the schoolroom stove

He lazed on haystacks in summer
inside his eyelids the sun's white blaze
listening to the skylark's reedy song
balancing chastisement and pleasure

And who was important to him?
his parents were like the gods
being beginning and end of days
drawing the year's shape with their rakes

His teacher who decreed he would
leave, being of more than average
fate; the girl he left behind, her face
remaining daisy-wreathed and pale

Some things he kept close, like
coins and portraits, and others
(patriotism, temperance, certain tones)
he shook off in bars and lecture halls

where fate or choice or history made of him
a man to be reckoned with, a man
who raked the shapes of men
in poems, and kept a wreathed muse

in his pocket. And when I, his translator,
stood by him on a stage once,
he touched me for money
and said his wife kept everything from him

and where was that prize, that prize
he was promised all those years ago
when he was driven by the fates
into the arms of time

THE LAST DAY OF YOUR CHILDHOOD

Yesterday
The last day of your childhood
We go up to the green hills where you are at home
Look down on the buzzards
And the sludge-coloured winter valley

The loosening of frost has released it back into decomposition
And no colour is intact
It undoes itself in algae
And wealden agony which is a paler version of the Slavic
Like aging in comfort

I'm walking the dogs
But in a cellar in my mind I am rehearsing a scene
In which a woman takes her child to a wasteland
And abandons it
War is coming and she is in flight

I'm wondering about the difference in sensibility
Between this woman and me
I'm wondering about the imaginative difference
What I would be if the air was never still
And the horizon smoking

But the air is still
Apart from my prattling
How I like to seize the moment
Hold words to its throat like
Future and luck and hope

Words that are countless and
Without value
Expended like shells into an area
In which all life
Is extinguished

The only chance of life here
The only small hope is in the repeated
Movement of lung and heart
Your willingness to forgive
The loosening between us

Sussex, 22 January 2017

THE TRANSPORTED

*'They led a group of women prisoners past. The women saw the men and
stopped. They wouldn't move. The woman guard leading them shouted:
'Come on! Get walking!' But the women wouldn't move.'*
— *Adapted from* Second Hand Time *by Svetlana Aleksievich*

Nearing dusk, a band of women passed
In padded jackets, rags wrapped round their feet
They saw the men, stopped, would walk no further

The men leaned axes, saws against their flanks
And watched as the guard prevailed upon the band
In vain, until at last she hissed in disdain

Animals, and spat and turned away. Like deer
Then they came. She to him, not pre-ordained
But more like atoms bond, drawn to pair

And each one fell towards another and it was done.
He placed his arms on her. Felt her bones
The matchwood girdle of her pelvis, her light form

Her face, the missing teeth, the lines of dirt
But shining, in the sudden grip of
Things beyond her, things she'd always known.

They had no time. He nuzzled her, pulled her in
And she put arms around his waist
And unwound the string he'd kept tied tight.

She ran her nose across his skin
He trembled, his hands were blistered thin.
Her haunches were as white as water

He was afraid to cause her pain
But seeing how she longed for him
He pushed his finger deep in her

Like meteorites
Falling through the dark – the ground gave way
He held her up. She was so very light.

He tasted sweat and something like leaf-matter
Fur, woodfire, her bloody snout
Her eyes level with his throat

Her flickering gaze. Saw he was lamed
Alive, but barely, like the first hours after hibernation
She opened her mouth, her tongue flamed

All projectionists know that a still
For all its perfection, cannot be held
It catches instantly, it will incinerate us all –

In fire the creatures briefly met
Swayed silently among the smouldering trees
Sleek as stones on river beds

Then fled. No longer of this world:
Motley pairs, scorched, but free
Seeking place where life might take hold

TEMPLE SONG

I was a saboteur, most of the women were
We'd spent months infiltrating the temple
Establishing relationships with the enemy
Making ourselves trusted, performing small acts
To ingratiate ourselves. We went to any lengths
To fit in, we were only useful if thought of as friends.

Like any saboteur, I did things I found hard to square
But I knew we were in it for the long haul.
I had to gain trust, make them believe in me
And sometimes that meant small betrayals.
I soiled myself for the cause, I hope you will see
It was not intrinsic, I was not me.

I worked for a money changer. I had dirty hands
I couldn't call the rates because my voice was a woman's
At night I returned the currency I had gained
And in so doing I maintained equilibrium.
My contact outside was selling horse gut
Spiralling out of a bag, white and profligate

She warned me that some crazy was approaching
Saboteurs know before the rest when the end is nigh
Our people are everywhere. The women selling mare's milk
The blind woman by the door. That woman with kids
Dragging them along the road, sweat pooling under her veil
She once passed on a truth that saved me for a while

Jesus was the crazy's name, I'll remember it for centuries
How he strode past security, lone Christ figure
Upending the tables, as strong as twenty oxen
Beautiful as Achilles, drugged, half-insane
Took ropes and bound them to make a flail
And the animals set up such a fearful howl

Three days, he said, it would take to rebuild
The media men pressed around his naked body
The walls had fallen in like an old rotten carcass
Water from hoses streamed over the little heaps
Of saboteurs, the last to flee, the first to die
And nothing left to remember us by.

INTIMACY

Just as when you unearthed a nest and all the tiny bodies
curled together touched the air and began their disintegration,

clutching like children or lovers, and still furred or feathered
but only for that moment, already extinguished, near extinction

beginning to break apart, just as morning haze disperses
when the sun tips the hill top, so much dust held in simulation

and now disbanded, I know nothing means nothing,
that substances transform, still some shapes touch more than others:

nestling things exhibiting proximity in death. To have a mouth
and press it against another's wing, to spread a wing and cover

over a sac of flesh, that fools me, makes me soft and hurt,
the ache shaped from love for what is not, and worse,

for what will be no longer, so mourning is double-vapour
rising from false intimacy between one corpse and another,

already gone, all of it, a loosening image of life and love
an attitude struck by the dead, their dry palms

cupping air. Even so let fools rehearse it while they have
breath. The shiver when a touch catches us unaware

you carrying me to bed curled in your arms,
the still-warm mess of sheets, limbs, hair.

ODYSSEUS WELCOMED FROM
THE SEA BY NAUSICAA

My bestie appeared in a dream and said
Your room is a slum, used sanitary towels
Curling on the floor, heaped clothes on the bed
Pull your finger out, girl, it's fucking foul.

So I asked my father: dad can I take the car
I've bagged up some gear for charity, I'll wash the rest.
And he knew right there what it was for
He knew I wanted to look my sexy best.

Dad laughed and chucked me the keys:
Take my car, sweetie, ask your friends.
Head down the beach, poppet, have yourself
Some fun, go for a spa with your hens.

Dressed up no one would guess our age
But on the beach we did all stupid stuff
Threw the ball around, played at chase
Took all our clothes off.

Sometimes we can get silly like that
I mean, without drinking, and on our own
Unafraid, somehow, did I say that?
Just girls, no pressure, just us, alone.

And then this man rises out of the sand
Naked as fuck but shielding his prick
Filthy with gull shit, smelling so bad
I literally tasted sick.

We're screaming, running from his reach
Because who knows what kind of fuck
Wanks off watching girls on the beach
I was terrified, I thought I'd run out of luck

I want to run like my fearful band
Streaming hair, screaming, naked as night
Twisting and turning over the sand
Like swallows in tangled flight

But something drags me back by force,
Curiosity, or pity for him, or even shame
Or the gods, who put their fingers up your arse
Leave their claw marks in your brain.

Or maybe just: he's a man, I know my place
Or maybe just I want to be chosen
Or maybe I'm a freak I'll be erased
My bare arm   I'm frozen.

First amongst femmes
Or slut without shame
I stretch out my bare arm
I see my hand far   far   away

Like it belongs to someone older
A little clutch of prehistoric fingers
And something fluttered on my shoulder

Feathery-grey,
full of hunger

Did I say I was never a victim?
Although I was riven like a sea-rotted hull
Although he took my life and flicked it
like a stone to the end of the world

I helped him with good grace
and inside I knew every complication
I learned to lie and it was barefaced
on my lies they built a civilisation

Rewind:
tell my father
to close the gates and hurry
fly like birds
from the wreck on the sand

But most of all:
don't listen to his story
close your ears   draw back your hand

PITYSAD

DREAM OF ODYSSEUS

Odysseus spent the day with the couple in their apartment, an unplastered room many floors up. There were no seats and no tables, but a smell of cooking hung in the air.

They wished to give him a parting gift, but they didn't have anything to give him. They looked around the room and shook their heads hopelessly.

They wanted him to leave, but they said nothing. He remembered he had to go. He should have gone long since.

They wanted him gone, yet they clung to him. He repeatedly stood to leave. They motioned him to sit. At length they all agreed that it was time.

He emerged from the block and it was dusk. Dusk on the plains lasts hardly a moment before dark blue night descends. Mopeds buzzed past, cars hooted their horns. Men, a swarm of them, were all returning home.

He was on the outskirts of a town and the road between the housing blocks was unmade. Not yet dark.

The purple sky, the warm, echoing air. He had to get to the centre of the town, to the marketplace where the long-distance buses stopped.

Odysseus knows it is dangerous to flag down a car.

His courage fails him a little. It was too late to go back, they wouldn't even open the door to him now.

You cannot trust the fearful, thinks Odysseus, they have no integrity. Fear is forced upon us, it acts on the body like a cancer.

He remembered he once found himself running with his right hand twisted in a spasm.

He stands motionless by the entrance to the block.

Penelope, lying awake, hears the ships
the cables clinking against the masts
the wind clapping, sees the bronze axes
glinting in the galleys

That day she climbed back into her car
and slammed the door against the wind
it was warm and drowsy at the wheel
still smelt of his deodorant

and beneath her in the bay
the ships fanned out into a wedge
of white-sailed cranes
silently, as she sucked a mint imperial

and if he'd turned and looked
she'd not have seen
and if she'd waved a hand
he'd not have known

She watched the ships departing from the bay
the water sparkling in the regatta sun
then reversed her car out of the space
and headed for home

Our shadows are as long as the life before us
here on the beach with the fire lit
and the galley drawn up out of the surf.

The kebabs are finished, the wine
is passed from man to man
and although Pitysad knows he is surrounded

by corpses, men who have gambled their lives
still he takes sweet pleasure from their company
their lewd jokes, how they hate everyone

and most of all themselves. A full belly
and a party and they'll see themselves out
because what is life for them but a vale of tears

and the empty seas are worse than Hades.
We'll get this, says one, and no need for change,
won't be needing it where we're going.

They wrap themselves in patched-up jackets
as the fog comes up the beach towards them,
and huddle round the orange sun of the fire.

We preferred brutishness to wiles
although we're not brutes, we're just the hungry
and night is descending now

but think how they barely ran from us
one looked at me like my own daughter
her eyes glistened as I brought down the axe

and all the wine in Ithaca won't wipe out that stare.
Fucking hell, Pitysad, if you won't berate us
at least play us a tune on your bastard lyre.

Everyone knows that the hotel is a dream of a little west. The manager knows it, the staff know it, even the man watering the palms knows it, and they are proud of the dream.

They all have jobs to do. The manager's job is shouting at them. He walks the public areas and shouts at the staff. Hey you, why don't the pipes work, it isn't a little west unless the pipes are working. The supply was cut a long time ago, replies the maintenance man, you know this.

The manager knows, but he keeps shouting. Why is the ATM empty? It isn't a little west unless we have money. There's been no delivery of banknotes, says the receptionist. Not for as long as I can remember.

Barman, says the manager, slumping at the bar, I need a cool drink. The barman gestures at the unplugged fridge. They are proud of the manager. They know he only wants the best for them.

Things go unrepaired. The furniture disappears. Wild boar make holes in the chain link fence around the tennis court. Little west was never finished, for example, they never laid the forecourt with flagstones and the pink dust lifts from the foundations in tiny typhoons.

I love the manager, says the barman as he takes a crate and leaves. Someone picks him up on the main road. The maintenance man lays down in a stairwell. The receptionist's sister wants to get her out.

It's too much energy to close the dream of a little west, especially when the earth will reclaim it slowly. The long grass whispers around the benches and their adjacent rubbish urns.

Odysseus is a complicated man. He longs for home, but when he reaches Ithaca he will want to leave again.

It's like physics, he says to the manager in the bar of the dream of a little west. He takes another swig of wine. All the energy of men, it degrades irreversibly.

And so the system comes to rest of its own accord.

… these hideous things
through a long absence, have not been to me
as is a lost limb to a veteran
but oft, in hotel rooms, or in the queue
for clothes and coffee, I have owed to them
long bouts of nausea and trembling hands,
felt in the blood, and scraped along the heart
and passing even through my traitor bowels
for sudden defecation: feelings too
of unremembered terror – *fuck, I shat*
myself this night and wake like one in hell
in this last portion of my worthless life –
and endless hopeless therapies and cures
involving CBT and ECT
just bandage wraps a man with wounds seeps through
to smear himself on walls. That dream of old
in which my GoPro, set to infrared,
my NVGs and their mosquito hum
are trained on unintelligible things:

Explosion – how the force lifts us like dolls
I lay my body gently down by his
and hoped the breath of this corporeal frame
and even the motion of my human blood
would be suspended – I desired to sleep
my body to become a breath of air

Instead I'm trembling, crying *fuck this, fuck*
the morphine pen won't open in my glove
I look into his eye and hold his stare

THE SHADOW PRINCE

Control it, Pitysad
                    says the woman with the ladle
take yourself in hand
                    slopping a half-measure into his bowl.

Outside it is warm and buzzing and jasmine-scented
and groups of women daub heavenly blue on benches.

I don't want to hear
                    says the whirlpool bath operator
try a jigsaw
                    says the snake-haired enema nurse

patients shuffle around in tracksuits and slippers
moustaches greasy with soup and stew
snore fitfully on the garden loungers
in towelling robes

Lord above, Pitysad, can't you lift your feet when I mop?

the women are as wide as they are strong
they're sensual for soft apricots and brandy
they're all widows or the mothers of dead children
they sleep with bags of dried bread and sugar
and they mop their eyes when they hear music

I don't care, Pitysad. Now show me your veins.

bald bards strum at night   the old war songs
the empty aphorisms   pleasant scandals
nothing proved   on the pulse

Pitysad is beginning to respond to treatment
when his friend the shadow prince bumps into him
on the Ocean Terrace:

you here?
amongst the mindless?
I've been a month in this place now
I'd rather be that man down there
blackened by the sun
looking for bottles in the bins

than this

All this black earth, reclaimed earth
he'd spent long days and weeks sieving.
Backbreaking work, first the big rocks
lumps of concrete, tile, flowerpot
put to one side for laying paths,
then the small stones rattling on the riddle's mesh,
the spikes of glass and plastic,
felted wool, bolts and screws, dropped into a sack.
Because it gave him pleasure to render something pure
remove all trace of humanity from the soil.
Its clean wet smell, its soft dark powder
under his bitten nails, his golden wedding band.
It was madman's work or the work of a saint
you could buy topsoil anywhere

Ready for sowing the day his conscription papers
rattled though the letter box

There were options: asthma, diabetes
a doctor in every town who'd certify
a club foot or a weakened lung
a hernia for a pre-negotiated sum.

He opted for insanity. Once as a boy
he'd thrown his model aeroplane
to the floor in a tearful rage –
the hours he'd spent on it
flicking a tiny squirrel hair brush
across its undercarriage –
and there it lay busted on the tiles

and his parents silent. Now
he took bags of dampened salt
upended them across the virgin soil.

The land was spoiled –
even the flock of gulls, drawn like a sail
behind the tractor, fell to the ground
and lay there, poisoned

He might have got away with it
but one day young Telemachus
strapped into his babyseat behind
said with such candour and surprise

but daddy does that mean you lied?

In the green marble of her bathroom
she lets the spasms of nausea overcome her
as one of her women holds back her hair

and another opens the taps
filling the deep bath, adding herbs.
She slides her bruised body into the warmth

and the marble kills the smell of despair.
Tomorrow she will appear in fresh clothes
and make coffee and toast

and the day will proceed
the sun piercing the blinds at noon
and towards evening

her women will begin their slow songs
and she will mix a drink and sip from it
and change her clothes again.

By six or so the suitors are arriving
driving slowly through the curfewed streets
and she has steeled herself

although, she reasons, better
not to be steeled, better to fool oneself
that this is pleasure or mercy

or the need to survive.
How she keeps them talking
like Scheherazade, handing round the drinks

how nothing betrays her, no flicker
of fear or hatred, the polished grace
of the wife of a statesman

even her kisses feel meant
her fingers' caressing touch
as the chosen one stands with loosened tie

or her smile as they all barge into her room
the way she makes each one feel welcome
as she stumbles, knocking over her loom.

R & R

Off duty, Odysseus often sat out in a park
a dusty place, neglected after years of war
one corner taped off because of an IED
and the cafes long closed

But still the nightingales inflected
sound from their pale little throats
and the trees offered some shade
although the sweat prickled his back

After a while the girls returned
to promenade in the evenings
clapping their hands, spitting seed husks
half-afraid but craving illicit freedoms

He'd be lying if he said he didn't enjoy it
he kept his book open on his knee
his body lolled, his eyes looked sleepy
but inside he'd never felt so alive

They streamed past, sometimes they doubled back
pouting and stealing little glances at him
teenagers with kohl on their eyes
and malnourished little bodies

and one girl let slip her tiny reticule
by the Greek warrior's foot
where the knobbly oleander
sent its glaucous stems over the path

He meets her eye and gravely hands it back
she colours, clasps her bag, moves away
and her friends rib her about 'her boyfriend'
and the Greek abruptly stands and leaves

But two days later he is back again
the same book untouched beside him on the bench
and when she passes, all alone
(he's not to know she's been there every night)

he speaks to her. It's fatherly concern
he thinks. A child out all alone
and enemies around. What are her parents
thinking? She answers: she has none

*

He brings her food parcels. Shower gel
lipstick. Her friends call her a whore
And one day he sees her bare shoulder
and lifts her thin hair and kisses her

He thinks: I could have killed her father
her brothers. I could kill her too
And she thinks: I love this man more than life
nothing else matters to me now

And then she stopped coming
When the city was sacked he sent
a man to find her, but nobody could say
where she had gone

A lad barebacked three hookers   but later he refused

to pay and got in a fight   filling one of them in.

He had to fork out 6k   in bail to be released.

The OC has forced him to tell   his wife. And bearing in mind

homosexual acts   go punished by death in Troy

a bunch were caught sucking dick   in a bar somewhere downtown.

Others got caught going twos   up on some hooker they'd found.

the lads have all been tested   and gated and banned from the malls.

community engagement is key,   a Greek spokesman said

we expect a lot of our troops   on and off duty, he added

STRIPCLUB

for hygiene purposes
he's asked to buy fake notes

the rules are
he can put them anywhere
and the strippers exchange them later
for US dollar

but it's like his eyes are bound
his body trussed

he gives the fake notes away
watches his men scrumple them into cleavage and g-strings

too much flesh and odour
too much profit and loss
for this thinker. He rests his head in his arms
on the melamine table. Smells disinfectant, sweat
wants to retch

Like that, head down, eyes closed
he hears
a voice, singing faintly
he can barely hear it through the throb of music
he cups his hands to his ears irritably
listens
it's calling him
it – she – knows him
she's calling him by his name
who is she? how does she know him?
how does she know him like that? from inside him?

like his mother combing his hair gently
like Penelope scratching his back with her small fingers
like Telemachus squealing on his shoulders
like the mourners singing for his lost soul

Pitysad, find yourself some tenderness

allow your hand to run itself down my spine

trace the tattoos the mermaid on a rock

Give yourself the gift of a shiver

He shivers, begins to lift his head

I see you
I see you and I can't stop my hands
It's not lust no
it's your own spine thrashing like an eel in the net
and wanting relief

I ache to finger it out of the smooth skin
release it to the pelvis like a bony fin
so it waves gently in water
and when you swim to me
it straightens itself
fish-limb
unspeaking

He's gazing around now

Now you raise your head
look at me

Your eyes are cataracts
and the barnacles have grown
on your teeth and your tongue

He looks, he looks, but it's dark in the club

Do you need your skin now
I ask you
to fly here now my dipper
watch me unpick your skin
open you so I
too
can be free

He gets to his feet
stumbles
he has no money
a bouncer pushes him back into his seat
his men half-rise

the voice is gone
but the memory hangs around him like an infection
a shameful infection
an itch
he curdles
he can't think
he can't snap out of it
the virus takes weeks to travel through him

Penelope is walking through the city. The streets are silent. The women never leave their kitchens.

Penelope's former lover, a businessman, wants to meet her in a café. Her former lover, a high court judge, wants to call her. Her former lover, a gynaecologist, wants to examine her. Her last husband wants to meet her where 'there are no crowds'. A writer she once dated tells her about a field of asphodel where no one ever goes. A man winds down his window and leans out: *where you walking to, whore?*

Penelope's former lover, the gynaecologist, is palpating her abdomen. At length he straightens up and washes his hands and dries them on a paper towel. Yes, he can help with an abortion. If it's really necessary. Does the father know? It won't be easy hiding it. He'd prefer it to be a home visit.

Penelope is alone in the toilet of a café by the docks. The sea air blows in through the open window. In the dark glass of the mirror she sees a skeleton covered in papier-mâché. The paper layered so thickly over the bridge of the nose and the forehead is newspaper from the years since he left. Revolutions, skirmishes, looting, arrests – headlines layered one over the next, all the letters melting into each other.

Her former lover is waiting for her at the table. He sees it's hard for her, but wonders whether she can use her influence with the suitors. *A contract or two would help*, he says, he wouldn't ask but his business is going down the tubes with all the uncertainty. *We've lived through a lot*, he says, emphasising the words with his coffee spoon. As he leaves he catches up her hand and kisses it gallantly, as if to suggest she is still attractive, there's life in her yet.

Penelope's former lover, the judge, calls her up. *A bad ruler is better than no ruler,* he says. His wife has asked him to intervene. *We're sick of living like animals. Don't misunderstand me, I feel for you. I am fond of you. But can all these suitors really be so bad?* Perhaps she'd meet him for a drink? He could take her out to his summer place.

Penelope sits in the café reading a book. For a while she reads and then she lays it on the table and looks down at her narrow forearms. Her skin is so thin she can see the sea beneath it, the tiny fish swimming between the fronds of cartilage and the sparkling coral bones. She closes her eyes. Luminous shivering shoals pass through her sponge-like lungs and her heart hangs weightless, twisting on its string in the currents.

The book is about a man who kills another man on a beach. She read it as a young woman and it seemed so glamorous, so grown up. But now she is an ocean she is indifferent to the ugly strips of shingle and their happenings. She lays her watery body over the surface of the world and it stretches to every horizon, and there is nothing and no one

Her phone beeps. She opens her eyes. A text from the writer. He's sent her directions to the asphodel field. *Dirty-white asphodel*, he writes. *Like a torn robe. I've got some pills. I've just finished my best work, so we could end it together. It would be beautiful.*

MEMORIAL

A monument to the funeral of a species stood
on the outskirts of a town
a bronze pair of muttering lips
in roughly-sculpted equilibrium, representing
the end of narrative.

It had dragged itself this far, old dog
and lain its bones in this ditch,
its furious intensity
succumbing to its own diminution.

It no longer drank its order from the jugs and streams of life
or propelled its wet self across the surface of a white-hot stove.

Memory was its life-giving fuel
and the subtraction of memory
its decline and death.

When those men devoured the fleshy fruit
fishing the segments from tins with their fingers

they voided all data
snapped open the backs of cameras and ripped out the film
set memory free to blow like the wind over the Æolian Sea
then chased it like the succulent pig
                    snapping its spine with a single blow

no homecoming drives us forward
and no sweet parting
sends us back to shiver in the past
                let us sing

                    our new song
of the biological storm
of atoms pulled from rocks
                    to replace those lost at sea
of the pebble's journey
of loss and gain
        and our fast lives
tiny explosions of sound   resounding infinitely
    infinitely unheard

and narrative flew into chaos
all noise no hurt
dispersed itself like slow black ash

muttering

WAR CRIMES

There are many ways to sack a city, says Odysseus
but when a city has been under siege for ten years
its will is soft like soap, disparate like flakes of soot.
Its people stumble over the sunlit squares
where once, years ago, the government ordered assembly
and loaded up the infirm, the foreign, in trucks.

Now the dead lie with certainty
in their mass pits and this is considered luck
by the living who wander the banks of Lethe
their possessions gone, their books buried or spurned
their windows glassless, they sleep wrapped in winding cloth,
make heatless fires of paper when all else is burnt.

But they hang on life with the intentness of a spider
they have nothing left to lose, except that sticky thread.
A gentle push at the walls and they will subside
the city's magnificence from afar is no more than a web
tattered by the wind. There's little left to loot
the Trojan men and women are indistinguishable
they all wear dirty robes and worn military boots
their human instincts have shrivelled to a dormant seed
they lie and fight for any scrap of food
they steal crumbs from the pockets of the dead.

So we storm the city, install our own king?
convince them of our superiority with gifts of grain and wine?
ask the Greeks, crowded around their great strategist.
Odysseus hesitates. Whilst that would be a fine
gesture, he answers, I'm afraid the truth is this:

We go in with fire bombs and tanks
and we destroy every single trace of human life.
We leave Troy no more than an archaeological layer
in the soil of a pristine green hill, a wraith
and its people extinct: a few beads, a clay urn
the scorched contents of a girl's reticule.

Anyone who says differently is a fool
for they'll be back in no time
on our shores, clamouring for blood, killing our sons
and where we showed them mercy
they'll show us none.

LAST RESORT

Odysseus found lodgings in a ski chalet in the
  mountains.
The rusting legs of ski lifts walked across the high
  pastures, their connecting cables were unstrung.
It was summer and the pastures were filled with wild
  flowers and goats under the sun's lazy eye.
Piles of concrete tension weights were spilled here and
  there in the grass.

Most of all, it is silent here. The wind on the meadows
  blows the grass into a sea.
After the troubles no one came here, no one ever came.
  The roads were destroyed.
Things move on, it is always easier to start in a new
  place, thinks Pitysad.

He wanders along an old path and sits on a boulder.
Shed the old places. Shed the memories.

Be quick and empty like a winecup, passed from mouth
  to mouth.

On an island of olive and lemon groves I met a woman who was in love with Pitysad. She was sitting in a room with the other women of the island. A waiting room, bare, with long benches along the walls, and when she raised her face to me I knew it was her. I was shocked because she was an old woman, her face was lined and her long hair was white.

In her letters (which I had seen) she described wandering the lonely beaches and the coastal roads, scattered with driftwood, and feeling uplifted, but also deeply unhappy. I tried to tell Pitysad, I said *she loves you, it's plain to me.*

I felt sorry for her, but also ashamed I knew about this passion, because it had come too late in her life. She resembled a tree ravaged by autumn storms. I spoke to her, I watched her aging, naked face. She looked back at me without sympathy, without recognition, but reflectively.

SHADOW PEOPLE

How they are always to be found
in the dark compartments of trains,
crossing borders, or rivers where a border once
flowed, briefly-lit as the dreary bells at crossings
grow loud and fade.

All of them marked: missing fingers,
thyroid cancer, women holding handkerchiefs
over their mouths to hide disfigurement
men with trembling hands laid on their knees.

All with candy-striped PVC carryalls
filled with tights, or oranges, or sausage
or anything that can be sold for an obol
in a market on the other side

there's a hierarchy of wounds
thinks Pitysad, *I am alive*
yet I am of them

He declines their hospitality
the schnapps, the chicken legs

he speaks *yes, I've been around a bit*
but belong in this part of the world

is geography dead? they ask
are death and life now one?
they can't see him
prince of cuts, he covers his face with his cloak
and the shades cannot touch him
although they reach out with timid hands

pitysad man
whose friend the shadow prince
calls him all the time:

a month in civvies
and I'd rather be the lowliest
shitscrubber
than this

PITYSAD

I entered a city at night, Penelope
I couldn't tell whether it was half-built or half-destroyed
I ordered you killed, Penelope
as I felt your hips in my hands
your head under mine
as I stroked your hair
and wondered if you were still alive

I moved through the streets and they were silent
but I kicked down doors
I crouched in stairwells
and I saw you emerge
from blasted places
holding up my old coat
and looking for me

It was a cloudless night
and the stars were tiny holes
in the sky's blackout
beyond that dark fabric
there's a lit room
brightly lit
and although I can't dance, Penelope
we were dancing

I burst into a room
a few women huddled
clutching pomegranates
I thought they were bombs, Penelope
I swear
I thought they were
bombs

sweating in my nightrobe I go to throw back the window and hear the bell down at the quay it thrills through me being a sign that a vessel is entering harbour so I hold up my lantern with my hand around the glass to look out and notice how my fingers their shadows appear like octopus legs on the house wall opposite so I splay them and wriggle them like a child and laugh silently as the huge octopus wriggles its splayed legs and drags itself to the edge of the lit wall I can see nothing beyond of course hear only the black sea at night how it breathes and sucks like the old dog ssshh haaaf ssshh haaaf like that not like water not like the water from the tap trickling in strings on the tomatoes in the sink can it be the same thing that icy dark element that presses on the coast come and press yourself against me sea ssshh it's so hot at night haaaf ssshh haaaf the air outside is hardly cooler and I open my robe and I stand at the window and the heat pulses through me hotter than the sun my heart and ribs like a faulty old boiler watch tiny droplets of water appear on my breasts like magic like whey wrung out of curds and trickle down me as this furnace of a body burns itself out and the cold deep water not far away how strange it is being both widowed and married to a ghost not knowing whether the best of my life is it behind me or is it before me and does it matter where I am on my life's journey except that if I knew I might try harder but how can I in this strange fierce hot tent of a body that does not belong to me as the dark waters rise and fall ssshh haaaf a thing left behind a discarded thing but still worthy of love because all things no matter how small and worn all living things are worth loving because if we gave out love according to size or beauty yes I'd love that picture of my husband the warrior with hyacinthine hair but I don't even recognise him I am afraid all my desire for the ghost husband I carry within me will wither down on the quay when he appears and we kiss like the unfeeling and turn away from each other in disappointment but now with all his ghostliness I feel his body next to mine behind me yes I feel it he is placing his human hands around me around the scalding heat of me he places them on my breasts and yes I'd brush away all the hero all the myth I'd chip and plane away at the lying outer form of him to expose the worthless soul inside yes worthless and if he could only bear it I would take that insignificant thing and I would love it with all my own insignificance I'm insignificant but I've kept going I'm insignificant but I am not a myth I am an existence and I am so full of love

*

THE FALL OF THE REBEL ANGELS

They didn't fall. It wasn't a pillar of legs and arms
a downpour of limbs, a shaft of flesh
like a rainstorm, dark over the sea –

No, they walked. They shouldered packs
laced boots, adjusted straps.
In hi-spec technical wear,
fleeces, gaiters, fearless, the angels
dropped from mountain top
and picked through the debris of rock
hopped over pavements, sundew, grikes
down scarps and slopes
entering the world on the thinnest paths,
the G R s from the stars
the trails, the aura
of a rope team on a glacier
the scramble, the clumsy jump
the odd angel on a bog,
jumping like a man from clump to clump
of cottongrass, falling into mud,
on a seraphic arse, over stiles and gates
and shifting slate in drystone walls,
built before the world knew how to fall,
and bathing in tarns, marvelling at
lambs, napping under pines
walking, walking in angelic lines.

And when they slept their up-till-then
unused legs kept walking in their sleep, their dreams were
of rights-of-way. And even when the coming of
day meant binding feet and the dampness of wings

still they hoisted their packs and took their flasks
and walked and walked, lacing the land
with endless small tracks, which led
(where angels did not fear to tread)
down into valleys and snaking over passes
shining tracks, visible to the naked
eye, the man in glasses, the woman
holding a map. Daily trespassing
angels, angels who walked, and fell
from grace into mountain streams
forgive us our lack
of dreams, we have forgotten
how to rebel.

NOTES

The St Dominic's Press, founded in Ditchling in the early years of the twentieth century by Douglas 'Hilary' Pepler, produced a number of pamphlets and texts illustrated and written by the letter cutter and artist Eric Gill. This first sequence of poems in this book takes its name from the 'Welfare Handbooks', printed by the Press in the immediate post-war period. It uses material from Gill's writings, his diaries and notes, as well as reflections on his life, his sexual experimentation and the abuse of his daughters. The voice in the sequence is not Gill's – it is the voice of water *which is good for recording disaster.*

ACKNOWLEDGEMENTS

Poems from this collection have been published in *PN Review, Mal Journal, The Well Review, Stand, Blackbox Manifold, aglimpseof* and *The New England Review.* 'Pigment' was commissioned by the Newcastle Poetry Festival, 'Headland' was written as part of 'The Blue Crevasse Project' marking the centenary of W.S. Graham in 2018, and 'The Fall of the Rebel Angels' was commissioned by Candlestick Press for *Ten Poems About Walking.*